VOLUME 7

Silver Spoon

HIROMU ARAKAWA

AKI MIKAGE

A first-year student at Ooezo Agricultural High School, enrolled in the Dairy Science Program. Her family keeps cows and horses, and she's expected to carry on the family business. Deep down, though, she wants to work with horses...but...

ICHIROU KOMABA

A first-year student at Ooezo Agricultural High School, enrolled in the Dairy Science Program. Pitcher for the baseball team with the potential to be their next ace player. Plans on taking over the family farm after graduation.

YUUGO HACHIKEN

A first-year student at Ooezo Agricultural High School, enrolled in the Dairy Science Program. A city kid from Sapporo who got in through the general entrance exam. Now he's vice president of the Equestrian Club.

AYAME MINAMIKUJOU

Aki's childhood friend. Started an Equestrian Club at Shimizu West High School to compete with Aki. Sees Hachiken as a rival...for some reason.

TAMAKO INADA

A first-year student at Ooezo Agricultural High School, enrolled in the Dairy Science Program. Her family runs the megafarm. A complete enigma.

SHINNOSUKE AIKAWA

A first-year student at Ooezo Agricultural High School, enrolled in the Dairy Science Program. His dream is to become a veterinarian, but he can't handle blood.

KEIJI TOKIWA

A first-year student at Ooezo Agricultural High School, enrolled in the Dairy Science Program. Son of chicken farmers. Awful at academics.

The Story Thus Far:

Ooezo Agricultural High School's Equestrian Club competes in their fall meet... Hachiken faces his debut competition with a serious case of nerves, but thanks to Chestnut, he somehow makes it through! Landing fourth place in the Low Obstacles Class C event, he wakes up to a new, exciting aspect of horse riding. Without any time to rest, Hachiken throws himself into the preparations for Ezo Ag Fest...And so the man who can't say no became the man who works more than anyone else. Then, on the morning of the first day of Ezo Ag Fest... Hachiken collapses...

CONTENTS

Silver Spoon

ZAWA
TURN OFF THE FLASH FOR PHOTOS, PLEEEASE!
ZAWA (CHATTER)
ZAWA
THIS IS A SIMPLE RUN-THROUGH OF SHOW JUMPING RULES!
TAKE ONE!
ZAWA
ZAWA
ZAWA
AN CLUB SHOW JU

Chapter 54: Tale of Autumn ㉓

SHIRT: HABITUAL RUNAWAY

Chapter 54: Tale of Autumn ㉓

I'VE ONLY SEEN REGULAR HORSE RACES BEFORE. THIS IS TOTALLY NEW!
PACHI
PACHI (CLAP)
PACHI
PACHI
PACHI
PACHI
LOOKS LIKE IT FEELS GREAT!

DOKA (CLOP)
ZAKAKA
ZAKAKA (KA-KA-CLOP)
ZAKAKA
Toyonishi-san riding Ebisu.
Time: 63.04 seconds. No penalty points.
YES!
Next is today's guest competitor...

Joining us from Shimizu West High School, last-minute entrant Minamikujou-san, riding De Royal.

HO! HO! HO! HO! HO! HO! HO! HO! HO! HO!

BUWAWA (FLUTTER)

WHOA!!!

SFX: TOKO (TROT) TOKO TOKO TOKO

WA! HA! HA! HA! HA! HA! HA! HA! HA!

HO! HO! HO! HO! HO! HO!

TALK ABOUT FLASHY!!

HOW DOES SHE STAY ON THE HORSE!?

YOU'RE AWESOME!!

I KNEW AYAME-CHAN WOULD BE GREAT AT WARMING UP THE CROWD!

SHE DOESN'T GIVE A LICK ABOUT RULES, DOES SHE...?

BUBUU (BUZZZZ)

Over the time limit.

WHAT'S THIS?

HO! HO! HO! HO! HO!
I'M SORRY, MY ADORING AUDIENCE! IT SEEMS YOUR TIME TO BEHOLD MY BEAUTY HAS COME TO A PREMATURE END!
PACHI PACHI PACHI
PACHI (CLAP) PACHI PACHI PACHI PACHI
HEY, YOU HADN'T JUMPED EVEN HALF THE COURSE YET!
I WANT TO SEE MORE!!
HO!HO!HO!HO! HO!HO!HO!HO!HO!
PACHI PACHI PACHI PACHI PACHI PACHI
YOU WERE GREAT!!
THAT WAS FUN!
THANK YOU! THANK YOU!
YES, YOU MAY SHOWER ME WITH MORE APPLAUSE!!

HO! HO! HO!
VERY WELL!
HURRY UP AND EXIT THE COURSE!!
Yoda-kun riding Miyako. They begin the course.
かぱーん
KAPAAN (CLUNK)
NOOOO!!!

HEAVE-HO!
HUP-HO!
UHHH, WHAT WAS IT IF THEY KNOCK DOWN A BAR? MINUS FOUR POINTS?
THAT'S RIGHT.
HEAVE-HO!
HUP-HO!
脱走常習犯

IF ANYONE HAS ANY QUESTIONS, PLEASE ASK AWAY!

I'D LOVE TO TRY RIDING.
IS THE RIDING CLUB EXPENSIVE?
OOKAWA-KUN RIDING EBISU. THEIR TIME STARTS NOW.
HONESTLY, THE INITIAL REGISTRATION FEES AND THE YEARLY MEMBERSHIP FEES REALLY ADD UP.
OUR CLUB GETS TO USE THE SCHOOL'S FACILITIES AND EQUIPMENT, SO WE GET OFF RELATIVELY CHEAPLY.

IF YOU'RE ONLY RIDING ONCE IN A WHILE, IT MIGHT BE A BETTER DEAL TO PAY A VISITOR'S FEE INSTEAD.
Oh, oh, oh!
ZAZA (SKID)
AH, OOKAWA-SENPAI GOT ONE REFUSAL.
ZUZAZAA (SKRRSH)
UH-OH!
AH! AGAIN!
THAT HORSE STOPPED TWO TIMES, SO THEY'RE DISQUALIFIED, RIGHT?
OH DEAR.
Ookawa-kun and Ebisu are eliminated.
YUP.

たかた、たかた、
TAKATA (TROT) TAKATA
THAT'S TOO BAD...
たかた、たかた、
TAKATA TAKATA
HUH?

SFX: PACHI PACHI PACHI PACHI PACHI

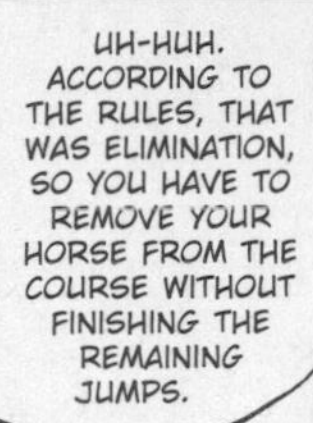

BUT IF THEY LEFT WITHOUT JUMPING THE FENCE THAT THEY MESSED UP, THE HORSE WILL END UP THINKING HE'S A FAILURE OR THAT THE JUMPING OBSTACLES ARE SCARY. HE'D LOSE HIS CONFIDENCE, RIGHT?

THAT'S WHY WHEN THERE'S FLEXIBILITY IN THE COMPETITION'S PROGRAM, LIKE TODAY, WE GIVE THE HORSES ANOTHER CHANCE.

I SCREWED THE POOCH!

GOOD WORK!

PON (PAT)
ぽん
PON
ぽん
OH WELL. WE ALL HAVE OUR OFF DAYS!
TO REASSURE THEM THAT EVEN AFTER THEY FAIL, THEY CAN STILL JUMP AGAIN.

IT SEEMS LIKE EZO AG ISN'T RIGHT FOR YOU.

YOU CAN'T LOOK AFTER YOUR OWN HEALTH. YOU DON'T KNOW YOUR LIMITS.
THIS IS HOW YOU PERFORM AT THE SCHOOL YOU CHOSE YOURSELF?

D...DON'T MAKE THAT DECISION FOR ME...
PUTTING ASIDE WHETHER IT'S RIGHT FOR ME OR NOT...
...YEAH, THERE'S A LOT OF PHYSICAL LABOR, AND THAT'S ROUGH, BUT...

...I-I'M GLAD I ENROLLED AT EZO AG!
ARE YOU?
YOU'VE ALWAYS LIKED STUDYING AT YOUR DESK SINCE YOU WERE YOUNG.
THAT'S WHY I BELIEVED SENDING YOU TO A SCHOOL WHERE YOU COULD DO PLENTY OF WHAT YOU LIKE WOULD BE BEST FOR YOU.

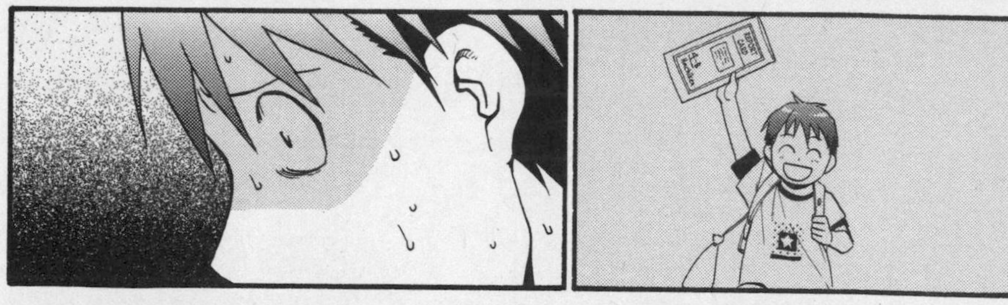

...AT PREP SCHOOL, YOU END UP SEEING YOUR CLASSMATES AS COMPETITION... WHETHER YOU WANT TO OR NOT...
I HATED THAT!
AT EZO AG, EVERYONE GOES AT THEIR OWN PACE, AND I DON'T HAVE TO THINK LIKE THAT...
I'VE MADE TONS OF FRIENDS I CAN ACTUALLY HAVE FUN WITH!

MIGHT THAT ONLY BE BECAUSE YOU THINK THE STUDENTS HERE ARE INCAPABLE OF OUTSCORING YOU...

...YOU FEEL YOU CAN REST EASY BECAUSE A PART OF YOU LOOKS DOWN ON THEM?

OH, HACHI-KEN!
ARE YOU OKAY TO BE UP?
SAKU-RAGI-SENSEI!
OH? YOU HAVE A VISITOR?

...THIS IS MY FA-THER.
DAD, MY HOME-ROOM TEACHER, SAKU-RAGI-SENSEI.
MY THANKS FOR LOOKING AFTER MY SON.
I'M SAKURAGI. I SHOULD HAVE BEEN MORE MINDFUL. I'M SINCERELY SORRY THIS HAPPENED ON MY WATCH.

YOU SHOULD BE.
I HEAR THE REASON HE COLLAPSED WAS FROM PUSHING HIMSELF TO EXHAUSTION PREPARING FOR THE SCHOOL FESTIVAL—NOT ANYTHING RELATED TO HIS STUDIES.

A SCHOOL IS AN INSTITUTION OF LEARNING. ALLOWING A STUDENT TO WORK HIMSELF TO COLLAPSE OVER SOMETHING OUTSIDE OF HIS SCHOOLWORK IS PREPOSTEROUS.
YOU ARE COM-PLETELY RIGHT.
IF I HAD PAID JUST A LITTLE MORE ATTENTION TO HACHIKEN-KUN'S HEALTH, THIS COULD HAVE BEEN AVOIDED.

BUT I DID IT TO MYSELF! SENSEI, YOU HAVE NOTHING TO DO WITH THIS!
NO, I DO. YOUR FATHER'S RIGHT.

YOU WORKED SO HARD ON THE PREPA-RATIONS FOR THE FESTIVAL.
I'M SORRY I CAN'T SEND YOU OFF TO ENJOY IT.

WHILE YOU'RE HERE, HAVE THEM EXAMINE YOU FROM HEAD TO TOE.
I WANT YOU LEAVING THIS HOSPITAL IN PERFECT CONDI-TION.

I'M LEAVING.
I'VE ASKED MISAKO TO HANDLE THE REST.
MOM'S HERE TOO!?

...DAD!

YOU'RE UNHAPPY THAT I CHOSE TO COME TO EZO AG... BUT...!

...THE BACON...

THE BACON I MADE...YOU SAID IT WAS GOOD!

YOU APPROVED OF IT!

WHAT DO YOU MEAN, I "APPROVED OF IT"?

I NEVER SAID A WORD ABOUT HOW IT TASTED.

SHINGO!

YOU CAME UP?

YOU LOOK LIKE A SLOB! I'D BE EMBARRASSED IF THE NEIGHBORS SAW YOU LIKE THAT!

HOW AWFUL!

THAT'S THE FIRST THING YOU SAY TO ME?

脱走常習犯

YUUGO COLLAPSES, YOU WON'T ANSWER TEXTS OR PHONE CALLS— I WAS WORRIED SICK!
AHHH, THAT'S MY BAD. MY CELL PHONE'S BROKEN.
HOW'S YUUGO?
I HAVEN'T SEEN HIM YET. THEY TOLD ME HE'S ALREADY RECOVERED AND AWAKE, THOUGH.
YOUR FATHER WENT ON AHEAD TO HIS ROOM...
HUH? DAD'S HERE TOO?
Visitor Information
Day
Night
HEALTH WEEK
fight cancer
be YOU?

KATSUN (TAP)
KATSUN
KATSUN

UGH.

I'M OUT.
SHINGO.
RECEPTION

YOU'RE RUNNING AWAY?

OH, YOU BET I AM.
I DON'T LIKE HASSLES.

WELL, I KNOW YUUGO'S ALL RIGHT NOW. I DID WHAT I CAME FOR.
SEE YA.

Silver Spoon

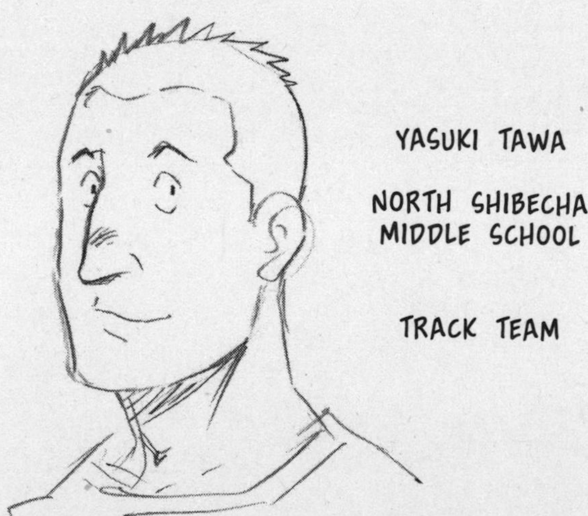
YASUKI TAWA
NORTH SHIBECHA
MIDDLE SCHOOL
TRACK TEAM

CHIRP!
CHIRP!
CHIRP!
Chapter 55:
Tale of Autumn ㉔

THEY SAID EVERY-THING CHECKS OUT.
OH? GLAD TO HEAR IT!

I'M TERRIBLY SORRY ABOUT THIS, HACHIKEN-SAN...
OH NO. I HAVEN'T COME BY TO SEE HOW MY SON IS DOING EVEN ONCE SINCE THE OPENING CEREMONY, SO IT WAS A GOOD OPPORTUNITY.
HACHIKEN, YOU'RE GOING STRAIGHT BACK TO CAMPUS, RIGHT?
HUH?
YOU OUGHT TO ENJOY THE SECOND DAY OF EZO AG FEST TO MAKE UP FOR WHAT YOU MISSED YESTERDAY.

MY GLASSES...
YEAH! I HAVE TO FIX MY GLASSES, OR I CAN'T SEE!!
I'LL BE BACK AFTER I STOP BY A GLASSES STORE!
ALL RIGHT. WELL, I'LL HEAD BACK TO SCHOOL FIRST, THEN.

I'LL GO WITH YOU.
THAT'S OKAY. I CAN GO ALONE!!
NO, YOU CAN'T. YOU DON'T HAVE ANY MONEY, DO YOU?
OH YEAH...
WAIT RIGHT THERE. I'M GOING TO SETTLE THE HOSPITAL BILL.

......

SO, SCHOOL...
HUH?

WHY DID YOU LIE ABOUT DAD SAYING IT WAS GOOD?

IT'S NOT A LIE! I HAD HIM TRY SOME...

YOU KNOW HOW YOUR DAD IS. HE BARELY SAYS A WORD ABOUT FOOD, RIGHT?

AND SINCE HE DIDN'T SAY ANYTHING WHEN HE ATE YOUR BACON...I TOOK THAT TO BE A POSITIVE SIGN...SEE?

I WISH YOU'D JUST TOLD ME THE TRUTH INSTEAD OF TRYING TO SPARE MY FEELINGS.

木商店
...I'M GET-TING OUT.
EH?

SIR, PLEASE LET ME OFF HERE.
HERE?

YUU-GO?
I'LL GO TO THE GLASSES STORE ALONE.
BUT ...

I CAN DO IT MY-SELF!
OHH, WAIT A MINUTE!
530
AUTOMATIC DOOR

GOOD-NESS... AT LEAST TAKE THIS!
TO PAY FOR THE GLASS-ES!

ぐしゃっ
GUSHA (CRUMPLE)

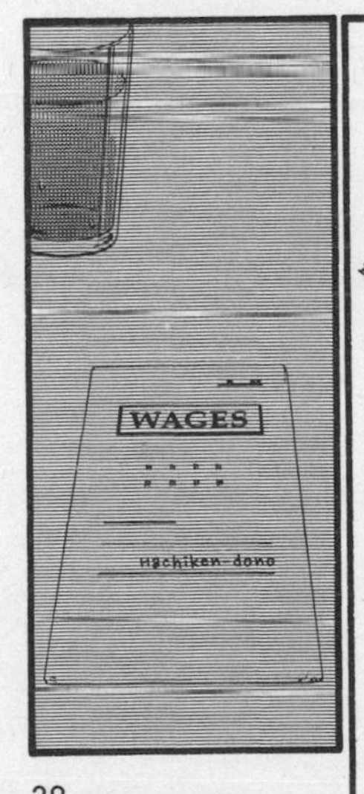
WAGES
Hachiken-dono

TOKACHI BUS LINE
....
....

...
DAMN
IT...
DOEZO OPTICAL
HOW
IS
IT?
IT'S
GOOD.
NO
PROB-
LEMS.
AIRFRAMES

HERE'S
YOUR
CHANGE.
Tohoku
Earthquake
Victims
Relief Fund
Donations
PLEASE
PUT IT ALL
IN THAT
DONATION
BOX.
EH?
IT'S QUITE
A LOT. ARE
YOU SURE?

Chapter 55:
Tale of Autumn ㉔

ROBE: EZO AG
STEP ON UP! WE'VE GOT KARATE CLUB SHAVED ICE!!
PING-PONG CLUB TAKO-YAKI!
ICE
BAGON (CRUMBLE)

I'LL TAKE FIFTY DAIKON RADISHES.
THANK YOU VERY MUCH!
I'D LIKE FIFTEEN HEADS OF CHINESE CABBAGE.
ALSO, TEN BOXES OF POTA-TOES.
SQUASH
SPINACH
Open at 10:00 a.m.
FRESH VEGGIES

SMOKED CHICKEN IS SOLD OUT FOR THE DAY!
THAT WAS FAST!!
CLOSED!
SOLD OUT!
HOMEMADE
SOLD OUT!

GROWING RICE, MOUNT FUJI, AND DOVES!
A FLAG OF PEACE AND LOVE FLIES ON THE GREEN WIND.
DOGAGAGA (DA-DOOM)
ZUDADADA (THRUMMM)
OOEZO ROCKFEST!

ZAWA (CHATTER)
ZAWA
ZAWA
ZAWA
ZAWA
ZAWA

HO! HO! HO! HO! HO! HO!

I'VE GRACIOUSLY COME TODAY TOO, AKI MIKAGE!! YOU'RE WELCOME!!

HO! HO! HO! HO! HO! HO! HO!

TRACKSUIT: EZO AG

JAPANESE DRAFT HORSE vs. HUMANS
蝦夷農
SHIRT: EZO AG

ZUUUN (BOOM)
大蝦夷農
NPK48

WHAT IN GOD'S NAME IS THIS!!?
A HUMAN SLED TEAM. YOU'VE NEVER SEEN ONE?
I KNOW THAT!!
GOT SCOUTED BY HACHIKEN.
ME TOO.
ME THREE.

OH! IT'S BEEN A LONG TIME, ICHIROU KOMABA.
YEP. WHAT'RE YOU DOIN' OUT HERE?
WHAT? DID YOU GO TO THE SAME MIDDLE SCHOOL?
IT'S MY FIRST TIME SEEING SOMEONE WITH RINGLETS.
WAIT, NO!! WHY ARE YOU STEALING THE ROLE OF THE JOCKEY!?
HUH?
BECAUSE THERE'S NO ONE ELSE TO DO IT.

THEN I SHALL DRIVE THIS HUMAN SLED TEAM!!
ME, BE A HORSE? IT'S ABSUR—
NPK48

BIN (TWANG)
THE POSITION HAS ALREADY BEEN FILLED.

GO!!

GRAAAAAAA

COME
Onnnnn!

THAT'S THE WAY! GOOO!!
SHOW 'EM WHAT YOU'RE MADE OF, HUMANS!!
COME ON, THERE'S NO WAY A DRAFT HORSE WILL LOSE!!

We're looking for challengers to form human sled teams!
Any team that defeats Black King will receive Nakajima-sensei's specially made cheese as a prize!!
ME!
OH! ME!
PICK ME!
I'LL DO IT!
WHAAAAT!!?

GEHHH!! IT'S TODOROKI-SENSEI, THE GYM TEACHER!!
DODODODODO (RUMBLE)
ドドドドド
DODODO
ドドド
MIKAGE-SAN, PULL OUT ALL THE STOOOPS!!!

GO! GO!
YOU'VE GOT IT!
WA HA HA
HA HA
HA HA HA

HA HA HA HA HA!

It's 3:00 p.m.
Ezo Ag Fest is now closing.
OOEZO AGRICULTURAL HIGH SCHOOL FESTIVAL
農高
PACHI (CLAP) パチ
PACHI PACHI パチ パチ
PACHI PACHI パチ パチ
Thank you so much for visiting.
パチ PACHI
パチ PACHI

OOEZO AGRICULTURAL HIGH SCHOOL FESTIVAL

Hokkaido Ooezo Agricultural High School

POTATO PICK
YUM!!
Pick your own potatoes!
¥100
Sold out!

THE RING... IT'S ALL GONE...
IT'S ALREADY BEEN PUT BACK...

YAP!

OH, HACHIKEN.
BYA (JUMP)

YOU OKAY TO BE BACK?
UH, YES. IT WAS ONLY EXHAUS-TION.
OH YEAH? THAT'S A RELIEF.

UM...THE EQUESTRIAN CLUB SHOWS... WERE THEY...?

じゃばばばば JABABABABA (SPLOSH)

YUP, IT ALL WENT SMOOTHLY WITHOUT A HITCH.

...OH.

I SEE...

EVERYONE'S DOING CLEAN-UP AT THEIR OWN STATIONS.

WE'RE HAVING A LITTLE WRAP-UP PARTY AFTER THAT, SO WAIT IN THE CLUB-ROOM.

ERR... BUT I COULDN'T DO ANYTHING!!

I...DON'T DESERVE TO JOIN THE WRAP-UP PARTY...

AH......

Silver Spoon

TAKUYA ORIBE

KAMISHIHORO NAITAI MIDDLE SCHOOL

TRACK TEAM

HNNN...

Chapter 56:
Tale of Autumn ㉕

FUI (FWIP)
ふいっ
!!!
SHE LOOKED AWAY!!
WHAT DOES THAT MEAN? "YOU'RE SO USELESS I DON'T EVEN WANT TO LOOK AT YOUR FACE"!!?
WELL, OF COURSE!! OF COURSE!!

AHHHH...
THANK GOODNESS... HE'S OKAY...
THANK GOODNESS!!

WHAT AM I EVEN DOING...?

I'LL GO.
I REALLY DON'T DESERVE TO BE AT THE WRAP-UP PARTY...
EH!? WAIT, WHY!?

'COS I WAS TOTALLY USELESS DURING THE MOST IMPORT-ANT TIME...
THAT'S NOT TRUE!! CELE-BRATE WITH US!!

HOW COULD I HAVE THE NERVE TO JOIN YOU ALL?
I'M LIKE HIDETADA TOKU-GAWA...
THE MAN WHO DIDN'T MAKE IT TO THE BATTLE OF SEKIGAHARA IN TIME......
HIDE...? WHO'S THAT?

...MIKAGE, ARE YOU BAD AT JAPANESE HISTORY?

I TOLD YOU, MY GRADES ARE AWFUL ACROSS THE BOARD.

AHHH...RIGHT... I WAS LOOKING DOWN ON YOU GUYS WHO GET BAD GRADES JUST LIKE THIS. I'VE BEEN A JERK ALL ALONG. OF COURSE YOU'D ALL HATE ME......
HOW'D YOU GET THAT IDEA!?

'COS NO ONE CAME TO VISIT ME IN THE HOSPITAL...
THAT'S BECAUSE WE COULDN'T LEAVE OUR FESTIVAL POSTS IN THE DAYTIME, AND VISITING HOURS WERE ALREADY OVER BY NIGHTTIME!

......
LOOK!

WE WERE ABLE TO FINISH WITH HARDLY ANY TROUBLE BECAUSE YOU LEFT THESE NOTES BEHIND!!
BI (THRUST)
YOUR NOTES !!

WE KNEW HOW HARD YOU'D WORKED AND HOW MUCH YOU WANTED TO MAKE THIS A SUCCESS EVEN WITHOUT THESE NOTES. SO WE WANTED TO MAKE IT A SUCCESS TOO, NO MATTER WHAT!
WE DIDN'T WANT TO LET YOU DOWN!
...SURE, WE WANTED TO VISIT YOU... BUT WHEN WE ASKED OURSELVES WHAT YOU'D WANT MOST...
...WE REALIZED WE HAD TO DO ABSO-LUTELY EVERY-THING WE COULD...
...SO WE DECIDED WE'D ALL STICK TO OUR POSTS...

SO THAT'S WHY...
OF COURSE IT WAS...
I FEEL LIKE AN IDIOT FOR SULK-ING...
YOU GUYS KNOW ME BETTER THAN I KNOW MYSELF...

YOU WERE RIGHT. I WANTED TO MAKE THIS A SUCCESS NO MATTER WHAT.
THANKS... FOR TAKING MY FEELINGS INTO ACCOUNT.

WHAT ABOUT YOU, MIKAGE?
DID YOU HAVE FUN WITH THE SHOW JUMPING AND THE DRAFT HORSE RACE?

YEAH!
IT WAS FUN AS ALL GET OUT!

COUN-TRY GIRL!
OH MY GOD! YOU DIDN'T HEAR THAT!! IT WAS "REALLY FUN"!!

HA
HA
AH
HA HA
HA

HA HA
HA HA
YAWN!
HA
HA
HA

OH RIGHT.

WE TOOK THE LIBERTY OF USING UP THE REST OF YOUR NOTEBOOK.
Campis
Guest Book
Feel free to share any thoughts and comments as well.
Equestrian Club

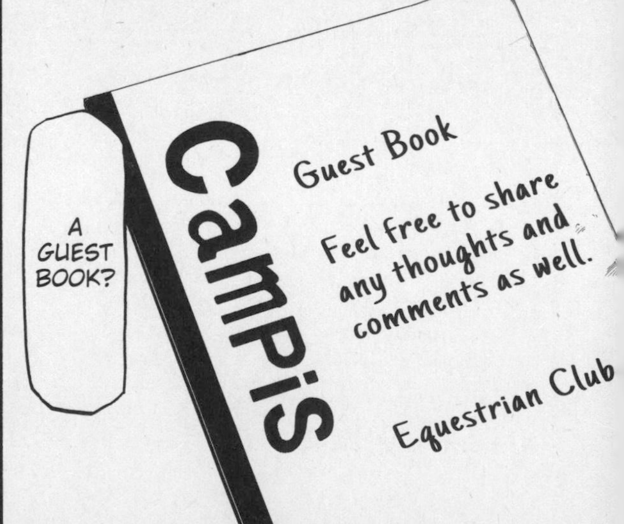
A GUEST BOOK?
Campis
Guest Book
Feel free to share any thoughts and comments as well.
Equestrian Club

PARA (FLIP)
パラ……
Campis
Guest Book
Feel free to share any thoughts and comments as well.

I was confusing show jumping and horse racing. I'm glad I learned the difference.

If you do this again next year, I'll come to see it.

The ugly horse was cool!

I want to see tHEm again!

The rules were easy to understand! Now I want to go see a bigger meet.

I used to ride a long time ago. This brought back so many memories.

PARA (FLIP)
THEIR HONEST, UNBIASED COMMENTS......
Guest Book
Feel free to share any thoughts and comments as well
CamPis

guess this is as good as high school students get. I expected something more
ssive. Disappointed.
OH MAN, IT REALLY IS UNFILTERED.
THAT'S HARSH!

THERE ARE SOME FAIR CRITICISMS IN HERE TOO.
HMMM...
WE'LL HAVE TO MAKE SOME IMPROVEMENTS NEXT TIME.
大蝦夷農業高等学校

AH, THIS ONE'S FUNNY!
WA HA HA!
THE GUY WHO WAS ON A HUMAN SLED TEAM, RIGHT? THEY GOT TO TAKE HOME NAKAJIMA-SENSEI'S CHEESE.
The last-minute entrant was fun! Her white horse was so cool!
"LAST-MINUTE ENTRANT"?

AYAME-CHAN CAME BY. SHE HELPED WARM UP THE CROWD.
SHE'S ACTUALLY A DECENT PERSON, JUST IN A REALLY WEIRD WAY.

I'd been feeling down because nothing good's come my way lately, but watching the horse working so hard to pull that sled kind of brought me back up.

Guest Book
Campis

JACKET: OOEZO AGRICULTURAL HIGH SCHOOL EQUESTRIAN CLUB

AHEM! IN CELEBRATION OF MY GLORY, AND YOUR HARD WORK SUPPORTING ME...
...AND USELESS ICHIKEN ...
IT'S HACHI-KEN!!

CHEERS!!
CHEERS!
WHY IS AN OUTSIDER LEADING THE TOAST!?

HACHI-KEN. GLAD YOU'RE ALL RIGHT!
WAI (CHAT)
WAI
SORRY FOR THE TROUBLE!
WAI
WAI

SHE'S CHANGED, HASN'T SHE?
WA HA HA HA HA HA!
WHO? MIKAGE?

BEFORE, EVEN WHEN SHE WAS LAUGHING, IT FELT LIKE SHE WAS STILL CONTROLLING HER EMOTIONS... LIKE, HOLDING HERSELF BACK.
BUT RECENTLY, SHE SEEMS TO BE PUTTING HER WHOLE HEART INTO THINGS— LIKE WHEN SHE ASKED RINGLETS OVER THERE FOR HELP.
I SHALL SING A SONG.
GIVE UP THE MIC!
OH RIGHT. NOW THAT YOU MENTION IT, SHE DID LOOK LIKE SHE WAS GENUINELY HAVING FUN DURING THE DRAFT HORSE RACES.

AT FIRST, I DIDN'T THINK WE'D BE ABLE TO PULL OFF EITHER THE DRAFT HORSE RACE OR THE SHOW JUMPING, BUT I'M GLAD WE WENT WITH IT.
RIGHT ?

HEY, HACHI. YOU ALL FIXED UP!?
HEYA.
SURE AM!
SORRY I DIDN'T FINISH HELPING WITH THE POTATO PICK...
HEY, DON'T SWEAT IT!
THE PIZZA STUFF WENT SMOOTH TOO SINCE YOU LEFT NOTES FOR IT.
IT WAS GOOD!
ARGH!! I WANTED TO EAT THAT PIZZA!!

WELP, IT AIN'T PIZZA, BUT SINCE WE HEARD YOU WERE BACK, WE BROUGHT YOU SOMETHIN'.
THE REJECT POTA-TOES?

WE'LL BORROW US A DEEP FRYER IN THE PROCESSING ROOM.
KARITTO (SIZZLE)
カリッと

DEEP-FRY TINY POTATOES, SPRINKLE WITH SALT, AND...
SEA SALT
2 Kg
TRY 'EM.
Thanks for the fooood.

HOT...
...AND GOOOOOD!!!
BU HA HA!

SFX: ZAWA (MURMUR) ZAWA

OHO? KNEW I SMELLED SOMETHIN' GOOD!
HEY. COME ON IN AN' EAT SOME.
THERE'S PLENTY TO GO AROUND.

AH!! HACHIKEN, YOU'RE BACK!!
YOU OKAY?
YEAH, I'LL LIVE.
TOKIWA, I HEARD YOU'RE THE ONE WHO CALLED THE AMBULANCE? THANKS.
I'M GONNA GO TELL EVERYBODY YOU'RE BACK!
HUH? COME TO THINK OF IT, WHERE'S NAKAJIMA-SENSEI?
I HAVEN'T SEEN HIM.

EVERY LAST CRUMB OF HIS CHEESE WAS TAKEN AWAY FOR THE HUMAN SLED TEAM PRIZES.

Silver Spoon

Chapter 57:

Tale of Autumn ㉖

EITA NINOMIYA

TOYOKORO
HARUNIRE MIDDLE
SCHOOL

SOCCER TEAM

Ezo Ag Fest is a wrap!
Great work!

SIGN: OOEZO AGRICULTURAL HIGH SCHOOL STUDENT DORMS

SO, HACHIKEN, I HEAR IT WAS ONLY EXHAUSTION?

YES, SIR. I'M SORRY FOR THE WORRY.

I'M HERE TO GET MY CELL PHONE. IT WAS STILL IN THE CABINET.

STAFF ROOM

When Spending Nights Away:

"Excuse me."

"Thank you for your time."

"Excuse me."

OHHH, OH MAN!

I HAVE A TON OF MISSED CALLS!

10/1 Sat
19:03
10/1 15:45
From Mom
Sub
Did you make it back to your dorm all right? Your dad's worried too. Please call once in a while.
Mom

Delete this message?
DELETE
CANCEL
KACHI
カチ
PI (BEEP)
ピッ
MENU
AH! THERE'S OUR GUY. HACHIKEN!
PATAN (SHUT)
パタン

WE TOOK FESTIVAL PHOTOS WITH THIS DIGITAL CAMERA!
CHECK 'EM OUT!

OH, I'VE GOTTA SEE THAT! HEY, THANKS A LOT!
ME AN' BEPPU TAG-TEAMED ON IT.

WHOA! THESE ARE REALLY GOOD!

WOW ...
KACHI カチ
KACHI (CLICK) カチ
KACHI カチ
カチ... KACHI
AH, IT'S MINAMI-KUJOU!
SHE REALLY GOT THE CROWD GOIN'. WHO THE HECK IS SHE ANYWAY?

SHIRT: HABITUAL RUNAWAY

......
FUNC.
SET

THIS IS...
THE VICE PREZ SHOW!! IT WAS A BIG HIT, MY MAN!!
WHY, YOU... I SHOULD HAVE KNOWN SOMETHING WAS UP WITH YOU TAKING HIM ON SO MANY WALKS! YOU WERE TRAINING HIM FOR THIS!?
HE MADE US BIG BUCKS!!!
じゃらん
JARAN (CLINK)

NOW YOU WON'T HAFTA WORRY 'BOUT FEEDIN' VICE PREZ FOR A LITTLE WHILE. LUCKY YOU, HACHI.
......
ずっしり
ZUSSHIRI (SAG)
NICE ONE, TOKIWA.

138
A Hajime Nishikawa
D Yuugo Hachiken
C Tarou Beppu
WHAT THE HECK? IT'S ALL PHOTOS OF FOOD AFTER THIS POINT.
BET BEPPU TOOK THESE ONES.

OH! THE DRAFT HORSE RACE!
カチ
KACHI (CLICK)
YEAH... A HUGE HORSE IN FULL GEAR LOOKS PRETTY COOL.

OH WOW. THERE'S A PRETTY BIG CROWD!
KACHI
カチ
KACHI
カチ
THEY MUST HAVE TRIED HARD TO GET WORD OUT.

TODOROKI-SENSEI!? OH MY GOD!! HOW!?
WHAT IS HE, A HUMAN TRACTOR!?
Gumon
BFF!

MIKAGE'S SERIOUSLY HANDLING THAT GIANT HORSE.
SHE'S REALLY AMAZING...
WHOAAA...
KACHI
KACHI
カチカチ

Gumon

THAT'S GREAT ...
SNIFF...
SHE LOOKS REALLY HAPPY...

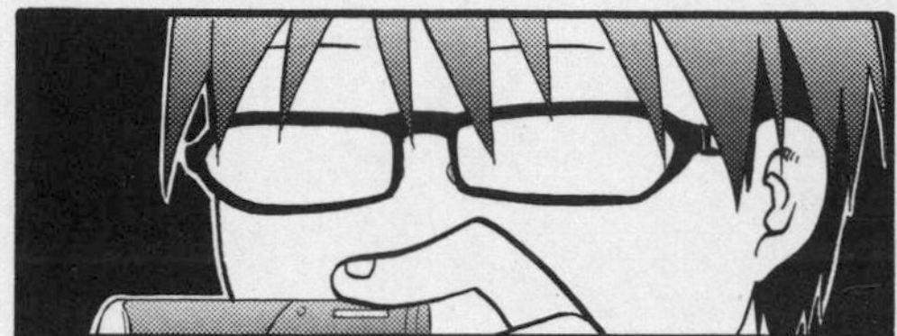

GRAAH!! YOU VISITOR CREEP!!
A COUPLES PHOTO WITH MIKAGE GIVING YOU A GREAT SMILE!? WHY, YOUUUU!!!

DELETE!!
KACHI (CLICK)
カチ!
DUDE! QUIT DELETING THE PHOTOS WE TOOK WITHOUT ASKING!!

IS IT
JUST
ME...

OH
YEAH...

...OR HAS EVERYONE BEEN EXTRA-FLIRTY SINCE THE FESTIVAL ENDED?
WELL, DUH.

A FESTIVAL EVENT IS A GOLDEN OPPORTU-NITY FOR SNAGGIN' ROMANCE FLAGS.
ROMA ...!?

COME TO THINK OF IT, MY PROMISE TO GO OUT WITH MIKAGE...
IT WON'T BE SCRAPPED BECAUSE OF THAT WHOLE MESS, RIGHT!?

YOU KIDS STOP PLAYING AROUND AND GET YOUR-SELVES TO BED.
YES, SIR.
GOOD NIGHT.

MI-KAGE ...
C'mere, c'mere...
YEAH ?

I'LL GO AHEAD.
OKAY.

H-H-H-HEY, SO, OUR PROMISE ......
IS IT STILL ON?
WHAT PROM-ISE?

YOU KNOW, UH...
WE SAID WE'D GO OUT, J-JUST THE TWO OF US...?
AH!
WE SAID IT WOULD BE AFTER THE FESTIVAL, BUT THEN I ENDED UP BEING TOTALLY PATHETIC...
I MEAN... I WAS THE ONLY ONE WHO GOT TO TAKE A BREAK, SLEEPING LIKE A LOG WITH AN I.V., SO, ERR...

...I WAS WONDERING IF IT'S OFF NOW...
OF COURSE NOT! I'M LOOKING FORWARD TO IT A WHOLE LOT!!

R...
REALLY, I AM...

......

OFF TO BED WITH YOU.

BYE! GOOD NIGHT!

YEAH, GOOD NIGHT.

ぱた PATA (TEP)
ぱた PATA
ぱた PATA
ぱた PATA

BOYS' SINKS (2)

WHAT ARE YOU DOIN'?

AREN'T YOU S'POSED TO BE RESTING?
I'M OKAY.
I.V. DRIPS ARE SUPER-EFFECTIVE. I FEEL SUPER-REFRESHED.

YEAH, WELL, YOU'VE STILL GOT DARK CIRCLES UNDER YOUR EYES.
URK ...

DON'T PUSH YOUR-SELF TOO MUCH.
IF YOU'RE IN OVER YOUR HEAD, DON'T HESITATE TO LEAN ON OTHERS.

GASHI (SCRUB) GASHI
がしがし

OH... RIGHT...
KOMABA'S DAD... HE OVERWORKED......

...YEAH... OKAY.
THANKS.
I'LL WATCH MY HEALTH. I MEAN IT.
SURE.
PTOO! GRGL, GRGL, GRGL...

YOU CAN'T LOOK AFTER YOUR OWN HEALTH. YOU DON'T KNOW YOUR LIMITS.

I HAVEN'T SAID A WORD ABOUT HOW IT TASTED.

RUNNING AWAY IN ORDER TO LIVE IS FINE.

YEAH. I'M GLAD I RAN HERE.
I LOVE THIS SCHOOL AND MY FRIENDS HERE.
I WON'T REGRET RUNNING AWAY ANYMORE.

BUT IN MY CASE, IT'S NOT AS IF THE PROBLEMS I LEFT BEHIND HAVE JUST GONE AWAY, PRINCIPAL...

SAPPORO IS WHAT, TWO AN' A HALF HOURS BY EXPRESS TRAIN?
LIKE WE WOULD GO ON SOME-THING SO EXPEN-SIVE.
THEY'D RENT BUSES, DUH.
HEY, IF WE GET TO GO TO SAPPORO, SHOW US AROUND, HACHIKEN.
SURE, BUT WE'VE GOT BEARS IN THE CITY TOO, Y'KNOW.

SAP-PORO CLOCK TOWER!
HITSU-JIGAOKA HILL!
ODORI PARK!
ALL RIGHT, SETTLE DOWN. IT'S NOT FOR FUN!

ざわ
ZAWA (CHATTER)
ざわ
ZAWA
ざわ
ZAWA
Sapporo City Maruyama Athletic Stadiums

札幌市円山球場
FIGHT
SIGN: SAPPORO CITY MARUYAMA BASEBALL STADIUM
The Hokkaido High School Baseball Alliance brings you...
...the Hokkaido Region Fall High School Baseball Tournament. We will now begin the opening ceremonies.
SHIRT: SAPPORO VOCATIONAL
札実
E

Silver Spoon

AYAME MINAMIKUJOU
SHIMIZU FIRST MIDDLE SCHOOL
CURRENTLY ATTENDING SHIMIZU WEST HIGH SCHOOL

Chapter 58:

Tale of Autumn ㉗

THAT WAS SERIOUSLY HEAVY!
DIDJA COME TO UNDER-STAND HOW INCREDIBLE HORSES ARE?
YEAH!

AIKAWA, THIS IS MIKAGE'S UNCLE.
YOU KNOW, THE ONE WHO LET US SEE THE BAN'EI HORSE CLINIC.
AIKAWA-KUN WANTS TO BE A VETERI-NARIAN.
OHHH, RIGHT! THEY TOLD ME ABOUT YOU!
HELLO, SIR.

Y'ALL SHOULD COME DOWN FOR ANOTHER LITTLE FIELD TRIP. I'LL SHOW YA AROUND.
AWE-SOME!
CAN I COME TOO!?

WELL, HELLO, MIKAGE-SAN.
HOWDY, PRINCIPAL.
I CAME BY TO COLLECT THE SLEDS.

THANKS TO YOUR HELP, THE HUMAN SLED TEAM WAS A HUGE HIT TOO. THANKS VERY MUCH.
AH SHUCKS. I'M HAPPY TO HELP ANYTIME, IF YOU'RE FINE WITH THIS OLD EQUIP-MENT.
I DON'T WANT DRAFT HORSE RACE CULTURE TO DISAPPEAR, Y'SEE.

WHERE IS NAKA-JIMA-SENSEI ?
AH, THAT'S RIGHT.

NAKAJIMA-SENSEI IS TAKING TIME OFF FOR HEALTH REASONS...
...SO I'LL BE OVERSEEING EQUESTRIAN CLUB FOR A LITTLE WHILE.

UH-OH.
IS SENSEI OKAY?
SO AS FOR TODAY'S MEETING...
...THE HORSES ARE TIRED FROM EZO AG FEST TOO, SO WE'LL TAKE THE DAY OFF.

THAT IS ALL!
......NOW I HAVE ABSOLUTELY NOTHING UNTIL EVENING STABLE DUTY......
WELL, DARN! NOW THE REST OF MY DAY IS TOTALLY FREE!
OOKAWA-SENPAI, WHAT ABOUT YOUR JOB-HUNTING?

YOU STILL HAVEN'T FOUND FUTURE EMPLOYMENT?
NO, SIR!
HUH! MAYBE YOU'RE CURSED!
NIKO (GRIN)
WHY AND BY WHO?

WHY DON'T YOU TRY PRAYING AT A SHRINE?
TURNIN' TO THE GODS, HUUUH ...?
WHAT'S THE BIGGEST SHRINE IN THIS AREA?
IF YER GOIN' TO A SHRINE, YOU OUGHTA SEE OOEZO SHRINE.
STOP AND GO!
THE WISH PLAQUES ARE HORSE-SHAPED. IT'S A NICE TOUCH!
A PERFECT FIT FOR YOU EQUESTRIAN CLUB KIDS!

AH.

Chapter 58: Tale of Autumn ㉗

HACHIKEN HERE. I'M LEAVING CAMPUS.
MIKAGE HERE. I'M GOING OUT TOO.
ALL RIGHTY. HAVE FUN.

ガラ GARA (SLIDE)
ガラ GARA
ガラ GARA
WHAT'S THIS, WHAT'S THIS, WHAT'S THIS!? WHERE ARE YOU TWO GOIIIIIN' !!?

YOU GOIN' SOME-WHERE FUUUN!?
COUNT ME INNN!!
ZASSHAAAAAAAAAA (SWOOSH)
ざっしゃああ
AH...!

GO, HACHIKEN! NOW!!
HUH!? WHUH!?
GWAAAAAAAH!
HACHIKEN-KUN, LET'S GO!!
THE BUS WILL NOW DEPART.
BUS STOP
EZO AG DORMS
PUSHUUU (PSHHT)

OOEZO SHRINE
WHOA ...
IT'S QUIET AND NICE...

SAWA (RUSTLE)
SAWA
サワ
サワ…

I THOUGHT IT MIGHT BE TOO OLD-FASHIONED, BUT PLACES LIKE THIS ARE CALMING. I CAN DIG IT.
PLUS, IT'S CHEAP.
RIGHT?

UHHHH... I'M HERE TO PRAY FOR MY UNIVERSITY ENTRANCE EXAMS.
I'M PRAYING FOR A JOB.

WE WANTED TO SEE THE HORSE-SHAPED PLAQUES.
WE WERE BORED, SO WE TAGGED ALONG.

ERRR... HEY... SORRY.
REALLY DIDN'T READ THE MOOD THERE.
NOPE, I'M USED TO IT...
HEH...

WELL, IT'S FUN TO HANG OUT IN A BIG GROUP.
YUP.
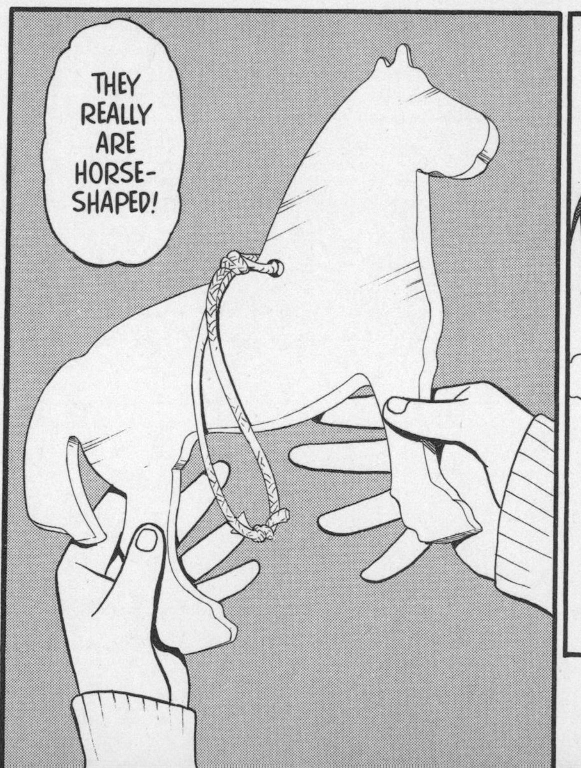
THEY REALLY ARE HORSE-SHAPED!

FORTUNE SLIPS ¥50
EXORCISMS
If receiving an exorcism, please step inside.
SO CUTE!
AND IT'S A DRAFT HORSE... YOU CAN REALLY FEEL THAT LOCAL FLAVOR...

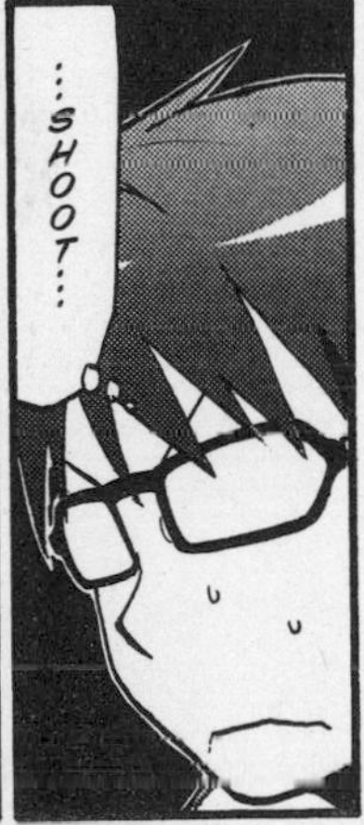
...SHOOT...

MOCKEE
NOW THAT I'VE SAT DOWN TO WRITE A WISH, I'VE GOT...
...NOTHING!!!

I DON'T HAVE ANY DREAMS, AND IT'D SEEM KIND OF GREEDY TO WRITE SOMETHING I WANT.
GET INTO FARM SCHOOL!!
KIMURA
better at it.
BUT I'D BE AN IDIOT TO HANG UP A WISH PLAQUE THAT SAYS I WANT TO BE THIS OR THAT WITH MIKAGE TOO...!!
May my family be healthy.

MMMM....
SHOULD I GO WITH HEALTH...? THAT'S SAFE...
NO, THAT'S LIKE AN OLD MAN!
OOEZO SHRINE

WHAT DID YOU WRITE?
"MAY WE WIN AT THE NEXT COMPETITION."

COMPETITION ......

かきゅ かきゅ
KAKYU (SQUEAK) KAKYU
かき かき
KAKI (SCRIBL) KAKI

...WHAT DID YOU WRITE?
HM? HOW ABOUT YOU?

WA HA HA HA HA HA HA!!
AH HA HA HA HA HA!!
?

AH HA HA!
HEE HEE HEE!

HAPPY PEOPLE CAN ALL GO EXPLODE INTO SMITH-EREENS.
LOVE CHARMS
THEY DO SELL LOVE CHARMS, OOKAWA.

AIKAWA, WHAT DID YOU WRITE?
I HAD TO GO WITH "MAY I BE ABLE TO BECOME A VET."

HOW COME YOU DECIDED TO BECOME A VET WHEN YOU CAN'T HANDLE BLOOD?
IT'S THE OTHER WAY 'ROUND.
WAAH!
IT'S SO OPEN!

I'VE WANTED TO BE A VET SINCE I WAS A LITTLE KID.
BUT IN GRADE SCHOOL, BLOOD STARTED TO MAKE ME WOOZY.
OH YEAH ...?

I GOT CARRIED AWAY AND WENT TO WATCH THIS AWFUL SURGERY ON A COW AND ENDED UP TRAUMATIZING MYSELF.
FOUND A BALL!
PASS! PASS!

OH, I GET IT. SO IT STARTED WITH YOU LIKING IT, AND YOU THEN YOU SAW THE REALITY OF IT...
YUP, EXACTLY. REALITY KNOCKED ME DOWN. I WAS SO DEJECTED.
FOR A LITTLE WHILE, I WASN'T ABLE TO EAT MEAT.

BUT EVEN SO, I COULDN'T COM-PLETELY GIVE UP ON MY GOAL.

I CAN'T CHANGE MY FEELINGS, YOU KNOW?
IT'S NOT A LOGICAL THING, LIKE WHETHER I'M SUITED FOR IT OR NOT.

YEAH ......

THOSE FEELINGS YOU JUST CAN'T HELP...I THINK...THOSE ARE THE REAL DREAMS...

I'M A LOT LIKE YOU TOO.

I ALWAYS LIKED STUDYING, BUT REALITY WORE ME DOWN....

BUT RECENTLY, I'VE REALIZED THAT I STILL LIKE STUDYING......

THE DIFFERENCE BETWEEN US IS THAT I HIT A DEAD END THERE. I'M NOT FINDING THE THING I OUGHT TO BECOME.

WA HA HA!

IF YOU THINK OF IT LESS AS A DEAD END AND MORE LIKE "I COULD BECOME ANYTHING FROM HERE ON OUT," DOESN'T THAT FEEL MORE EXCITING?

ME, MY DREAM IS TOO CEMENTED. THERE'S ONLY ONE PATH FOR ME.

BUT YOUR DREAM EXTENDS FROM HERE TO INFINITY.

We have a player substi-tution.
Ooezo Agricultural High School swaps out their pitcher Yamakoshi-kun for...
TEAM
EZO AG
N. TOKAI
R

... Komaba-kun.

SHIRT: OOEZO AG

Silver Spoon

TAROU BEPPU

OBIHIRO AIRPORT SOUTH TOWN MIDDLE SCHOOL

FOOD SCIENCE PROGRAM

HE'S PUT ON MORE WEIGHT SINCE STARTING HIGH SCHOOL.

Chapter 59:

Tale of Autumn ㉘

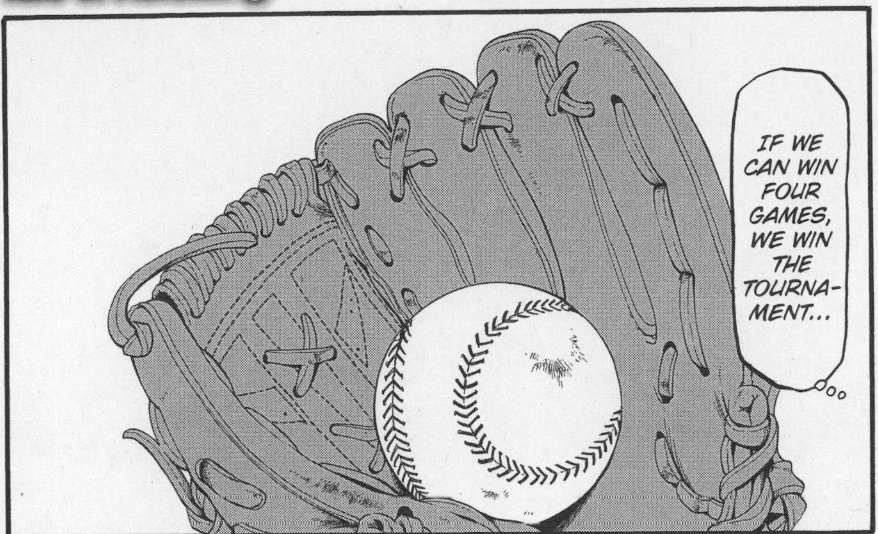

SHIRT: OOEZO AG

GU
(STRETCH)
GU

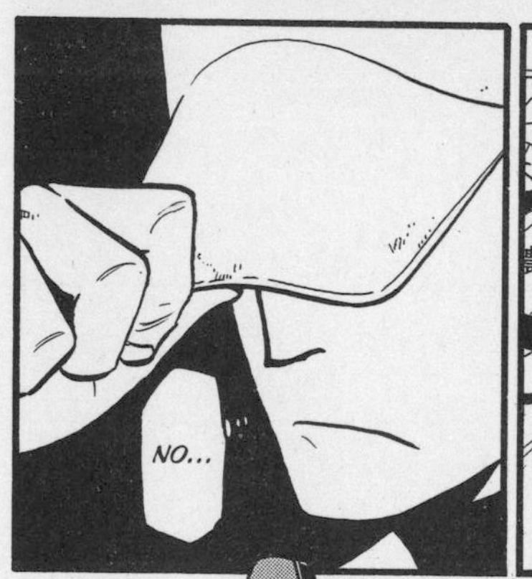
NO...

IT'S ONLY FOUR GAMES !!

WE'RE GONNA...

...WIN!!!

GO (WHOOM)

DODODODODODODODODO
(RRRRRUMBLE)

SFX: DORURURU (VRRRRM), GAGAGAGAGA (SCRAPE) GARI GARI

I WANNA SEE THE DRAFT HORSE RACE, BUT MAKING THE COURSE IS A PAIN!
I GET THAT, BUT I WANT TO ACTUALLY SEE US DO IT!
THEN DON'T GO COL-LAPSING NEXT YEAR, OKAY?
WE CAN MAKE THE COURSE, BUT THIS TIME, YOU BE ON THE HUMAN SLED TEAM, HACHIKEN.
NO WAY!! I'LL DIE!!

SNACK TIME
SALT

YUM!

OH YEAH. THAT ONE TIME NISHIKAWA GAVE ME A TRACTOR RIDE WAS PRETTY FUN...

SHIRT: EQUESTRIAN CLUB

......

SENSEI, THIS TRACTOR ......

COULD I TRY...... DRIVING IT?

ALL RIGHT, NOW PUSH THE LEVER FORWARD.
DO (PUTTER)
DO
DO
DO
DO
WH-WHICH ONE!? THERE ARE A LOT OF LEVERS HERE!!
DO DO DO

DO DO
ON YOUR LEFT. THE ONE THAT ACCELERATES.
THIS WAS IN YOUR FARM EQUIPMENT TEXTBOOK, REMEMBER?
I CAN SEE THE DIAGRAM IN MY HEAD, BUT MY BODY ISN'T KEEPING UP!
DO
DO

SUKON (PLUNK)
ACK! I STALLED IT!!
THAT'S ALL RIGHT. KEEP CALM AND START THE ENGINE AGAIN.

OHHHH! OHHHHH!
WHOOOOA!
GASHON (CLANK)
GASHON
SFX: DORURURURURU (VRRRM)
SFX: DO DO DO DO DO DO DO

YOU CAN DRIVE US ANYWHERE WITHIN THIS FIELD.
GIVE IT A SPIN.
FOR REAL!? YEEHAW!!
"YEEHAW"?
YOU'VE GOT A PRETTY GOOD KNACK FOR THIS.
IT DOES EVERYTHING I TELL IT TO, SO IT'S EASIER TO RIDE THAN A HORSE!!
SFX: DORURUN, DO (PUTTER) DO DO DO DO DO DO DO DO

OH MAN... MY EARS FEEL FUNNY.
GUWAN (DIZZY) GUWAN
IS THIS HOW THE MAIN CHARACTERS IN MECHA ANIME FEEL?
THE MORE YOU KNOW.
KAKUN (WOBBLE) KAKUN
GUWAN GUWAN
CAN YOU PILOT A GUNDOM WITH A LARGE MOBILE MACHINERY LICENSE?
BEATS ME.

ZAZA (KRAKL)

ZA

— is on the offense ...

Up in the batter's box is #5, Kiyota-kun.

He's had two hits so far today.

On the mound is Komaba-kun.

KOMABA?

IT'S THE ALL-HOKKAIDO TOURNAMENT!

ICCHAN'S PITCHING!
WHAT'S THE SCORE !?

KIN (CLANG)
It's a hit!
UH OH...
And it's...
...a fly ball to first! That's two outs!

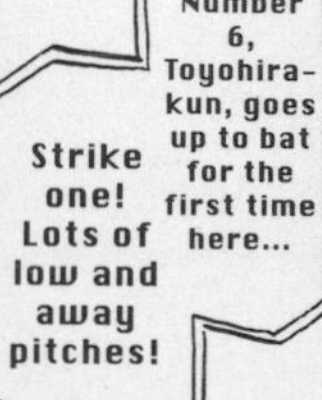
Number 6, Toyohira-kun, goes up to bat for the first time here...
Strike one! Lots of low and away pitches!

The second pitch... goes out of the strike zone. That's a ball.

On to pitch three ... Foul!
The fourth pitch...... another foul!

Ooezo Agriculture's Komaba-kun took the mound in the seventh inning, and he's holding back North Tokai's batters with very few pitches.
He pitches at a good pace too.
All right, here's the fifth pitch...

He strikes out!! That's game!!
This was Ooezo Agricultural vs. North Tokai. Ooezo Agricultural wins with a score of six to one and advances to the final eight!
YES!

AWESOME!
WOO-HOO!

FOR TODAY'S HANDS-ON, YOU'RE MAKING COW HALTERS.
LIVESTOCK MANAGEMENT
FOLLOW THE INSTRUCTIONS IN THE HANDOUT.
Halter

YOU CAN MAKE MULTIPLE HALTERS, FOR THE ADULT AND CALF SIZE.
BEGIN!
Yes, sirrr.

THIS IS TRICKY...
Halter
ピッ
PI (BEEP)
BUTSUN (VOOP)
LIKE THIS?

Ooezo Agricultural High School is up to bat in the eighth inning...

UH-OH. WE'RE LOSING, 1-2.

SENSEI, WE'RE IN CLASS...
IT'S BACKGROUND MUSIC!
OF COURSE!!

IS THIS THEIR SECOND GAME? WHO ARE THEY UP AGAINST?
DAISETSUZAN HIGH SCHOOL?
THOSE GUYS ARE REGULARS AT NATIONALS!!

DO (LURCH)

C'MON!

KIN (CLANG)

YEAAAAH!

URYUU-SAN'S RUNNIN' FOR IIIIIT!!

JERSEY: OOEZO AG

ALL RIGHT, LOOKING GOOD.

EZO AG 3–2 DAISETSUZAN

Ezo Ag swaps pitchers from Iiroo-kun to...

... Komaba-kun.

KIIN (CLANG)
HE'S UP!
WHOA!
KOMABA'S TOTALLY OUR CLOSER NOW.
FIRST YAMAKOSHI-SAN, THEN HIROO-SAN, AND FINISHING UP WITH KOMABA, HUH?

AAAAAAAAAAA
Foul!
KOON (CLONK)

...WWWWWW
WEH
Please watch out for foul balls in the stands.

Fly ball to center field...
Out!

GRRRRAAAAAA!

WHOA! THEY HIT IT ALL THE WAY TO THE OUTFIELD!
SCARYYY!
...!!
IT'LL BE FINE. WE'RE IN THE LEAD.
...!!

Strike
Ball!

Ball!
The count is 3-2!

KIN
(CLINK)

WAH!

SFX: PACHI (CLAP) PACHI PACHI PACHI PACHI

That's game!

Ooezo Agricultural High School moves on to the final four!

PACHI PACHI PACHI PACHI PACHI PACHI PACHI PACHI PACHI

WE WON...
WHOA ......
WE BEAT NATIONALS REGULARS ......

IF WE WIN TWO MORE TIMES...

WE'LL BE IN THE SPRING PRELIMS ...!

OUR WHOLE SCHOOL MIGHT ACTUALLY GET TO GO CHEER THEM ON...!
ZAWA (RUSTLE)
ざわ...

HUH? THEY ONLY MANAGED TO MAKE THIS MANY HALTERS?
WA HA HA HA HA HA HA
HOO BOY, THOSE 1-D KIDS ARE SLOW WORKERS. FOR SHAME!

Silver Spoon

HAJIME NISHIKAWA

NEW HIDAKA FOURTH MIDDLE SCHOOL

AGRICULTURAL SCIENCE PROGRAM

HIS FAMILY GROWS TOMATOES, ASPARAGUS, AND POTATOES.

Chapter 60:
Tale of Autumn ㉙

VROOM
OH. IT'S NOON.
LET'S BREAK FOR SOME GRUB.

DAD, GRANDPA! I'M HOOOME!
HEY. WLL COME HOME.
HEY!

NO CLUB?
I'M NOT ON DUTY TODAY.

DOSA (WHUMP)
ドサ
BASA (RUSTLE)
バサ
SUTA (PLOP)
すた
PI (BEEP)
ピッ
I'M HOME, GREAT-GRANDMA!

SFX: DON (BOOM) DON DON DON DON
Ooezo Agricultural High School vs. Hakodate Ryuuhoku.
KAAAAAH!
It's the top of the first inning. Ezo Ag is up at bat.
The batter is Hidaka-kun.
SO THE GAME JUST STARTED!

WIN, ICHIROU ...!

Chapter 60: Tale of Autumn 29

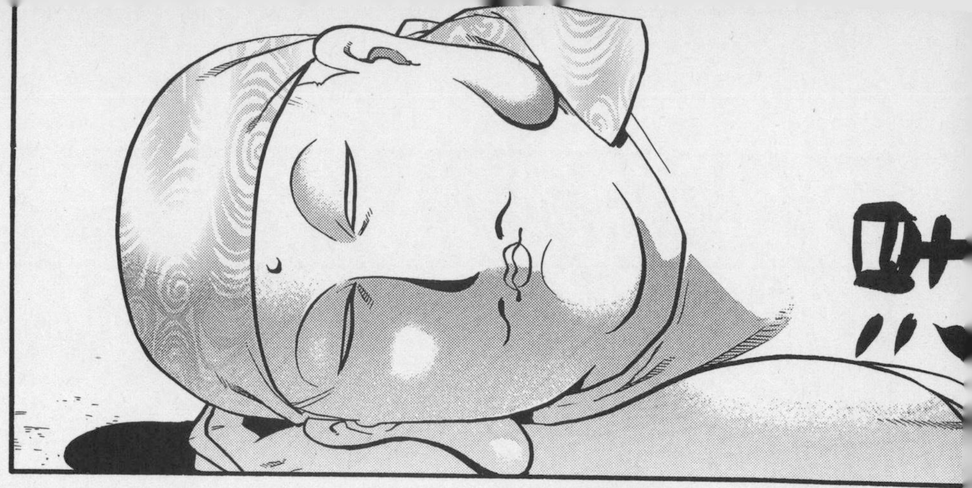

SHIRT: THE DEATH OF BUDDHA

WE CAME BY TO PLAY WITH VICE PREZ.
KAI (SCRATCH)
かいかいかい
KAI
KAI
AHHHH...
OH, OKAY... WAIT, VICE PREZ!?
YOU'LL SHOW YOUR BELLY TO JUST ANYONE!?

THAT'S FINE, BUT I'M DONE WITH STABLE DUTY, SO I'M OUT OF HERE.
SOWA (FIDGET)
SOWA
そわそわ
WHAT'S THE RUSH? GOT SOME-THIN' TO DO?

...AREN'T THE BASEBALL SEMIFINALS STARTING ANY MINUTE NOW?
SOWA
そわ...

OH!
OH YEAH!
IN THAT CASE!

MOOO...
MROOOO...

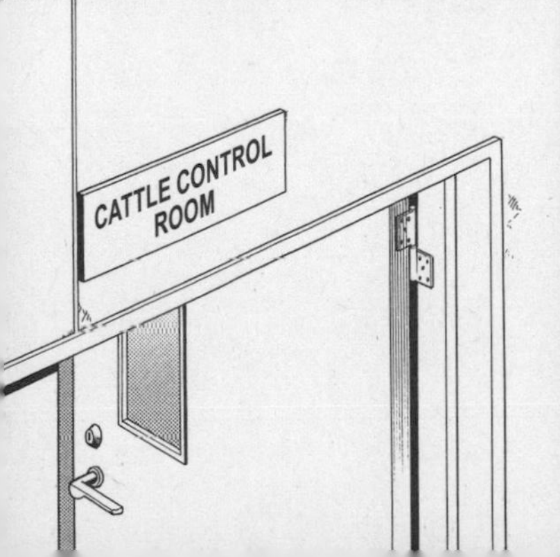
CATTLE CONTROL ROOM

HUH, PRINCIPAL? WHAT BRINGS YOU HERE, SIR?
EXCUSE THE INTRUSION.
ARE YOU USING THAT MONITOR?
THAT'S RIGHT. I'M WATCHING A COW WHO'S ABOUT TO GO INTO LABOR.
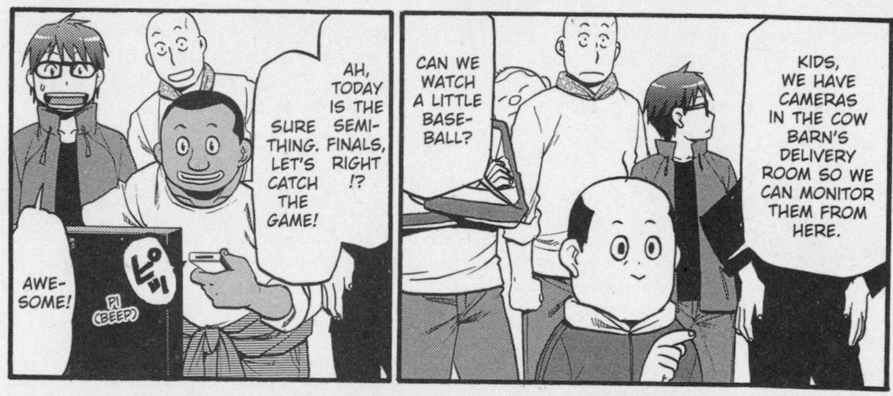
KIDS, WE HAVE CAMERAS IN THE COW BARN'S DELIVERY ROOM SO WE CAN MONITOR THEM FROM HERE.
CAN WE WATCH A LITTLE BASEBALL?
AH, TODAY IS THE SEMI-FINALS, RIGHT!?
SURE THING. LET'S CATCH THE GAME!
PI (BEEP)
AWESOME!

TEAM
EZO AG
0
RYUUHOKU
3
CRAP! WE'RE ALREADY THREE RUNS BEHIND!
WELL, SHOOT. WE'RE LOSING. I WAS AFRAID OF THIS.

ARE WE PLAYING A STRONG TEAM?
YUP. THEY WERE IN THE SUMMER CHAMPI-ONSHIPS.

I HEARD THEY LET STRONG BASEBALL PLAYERS FROM KANSAI INTO THEIR SCHOOL.
ISN'T ALMOST THEIR WHOLE TEAM FROM KANSAI?
CRAP. WHAT GIVES? THEY SOUND STRONG!

MAYBE WE CAN GET SOME-BODY FROM KANSAI TOO.
THEY CAN BRING THEIR WEST WAGYU CATTLE CULTURE WITH 'EM.
WAGYU BEEF... I WANNA EAT SOME WAGYU BEEF!
HOW DID WE GET FROM BASEBALL TO BEEF?
HOLSTEINS ARE PLENTY DELICIOUS TOO!

WAAH!

YEAAAH!
ALL RIGHT! NICE RUN!!

KIN
(CLANG)

HE'S RUN-NING!!
IT'S A BIG ONE!!

Ohh, it's...
...not quite!!
It's caught in front of the right field fence!
He's out!

That's three outs!
ARRRRGH!
SO CLOOOSE!
Ooezo Agricultural High School finishes the second inning without scoring any runs.
THIS IS BAD FOR THE HEART...
ドッドッドッ
DO DO DO (BADUM)
OH RIGHT. BETTER CHECK ON THE COW.
ピッ
PI (BEEP)

OH! THE CALF'S HOOVES ARE OUT!

ALL RIGHT! TIME TO GO, HACHIKEN-KUN!
BYA (JOLT)
WHY ME!?

YOU'RE THE ONLY DAIRY SCIENCE KID HERE.
MM-HMM!
I CAN'T DO DELIVERIES!!! I CAN'T HANDLE THEM!!! PLEASE CUT ME A BREAK!!!

WE'LL KEEP AN EYE ON THE GAME FOR YA!
NO WORRIES. GO ON, THEN!
WAAAAAAAAH!!!

RUNNING AWAY IN ORDER TO LIVE IS PERFECTLY FINE!!!

SHA (ZOOM)

HEY, WEL-COME BACK.

EZO AG 4-3 RYUUHOKU

HUH!? WE'RE WINNING!!

MAN, THOSE WERE SOME GREAT MOVES!

LIKE HOW WE SENT IN ABUTA-SAN AS A PINCH HITTER.

AND BEFORE THAT WE HAD THE BASES LOADED WITH NO OUTS.

SORACHI-SAN WAS ALMOST SUPER-HUMAN.

WE GOT CRAZY EXCITED!

THE FEELING OF BEING LEFT OUT FROM THE FESTIVAL STRIKES AGAIN...!!

DAMMIIIIT... I WANNA GET ALL EXCITED WITH YOU GUYS TOOOOO...!
WE'RE AT ONE OUT WITH RUNNERS ON FIRST AND SECOND BASE. YOU COULD STILL GET YOUR CHANCE.
...AND HE HIT IT!!!
KIIN (CLANG)

...It's a line drive to the shortstop! A double play!!
No more runs for Ooezo Acricultural High School this inning!

AWWW!
A TWIN KILLING !?
GAAAH!! SO CLOOOSE !!
AND THAT WAS A BIG CHANCE TOO!!
PIPI (BEEP)
LET ME CHECK ON THE COWS......

AH, THE NEXT COW'S GOING INTO LABOR.
DUTY CALLS, HACHIKEN-KUN!
GYAAAAAAAAAAH!

PURU (TREMBLE)
プル
PURU
プル
PURU
プル

BLARGH...

WHAT'S NEXT? THE FIRST MILKING AGAIN...?
NOPE, THIS COW KICKS A LOT, SO I'LL DO THAT.

...DOES THAT MEAN...I CAN GO BACK TO WATCH THE GAME!?
NOPE, NOT YET.

THE AFTERBIRTH FROM THE FIRST DELIVERY CAME OUT. CLEAN THAT UP FIRST.
AFTER-BIRTH...

WHAT COMES OUT AFTER THE BIRTH.
THE PLA-CENTA.
AN ORGAN.

ULP... HRK...
...!!!

WEL-COME BACK.
YOUR JOINTS ARE LOOKIN' WEIRD, HACHI-KEN.
AFTER TWO DELIVERY EXPERIENCES IN A ROW, YOU'RE A VETERAN, RIGHT?
WA-HA-HA-HA!
DON'T FRAME IT AS "EXPERIENCE IS EVERYTHING," FARMERS!
THIS ISN'T THE LOOK OF A VETERAN! THIS IS MENTAL COLLAPSE!

WAH!
ANYWAY, WHAT'S THE SCORE NOW!?
WE'RE WINNIN', 5-4.
WE'RE WIN-NING... BUT...
AH!!

Ball four! That's a walk!
HAKODATE RYUUHOKU
BASEBALL SPIRIT

It's the bottom of the ninth with no outs and the bases are loaded!
WHAT!? WE'RE IN A JAM!?
OH CRAP ...

Ooezo Agri-cultural High School...
...swaps pitchers from Hiroo-kun to...

KAH!
... Komaba-kun!

OH! HE'S UP!
STRIKE 'IM OUT, KOMA-BAAA!

ド DO (BADUM)
ドドドドドドドド DO DO DO DO DO DO DO DO
OH MAN, I'M SO NERVOUS I COULD DIE......
COMING IN TO PITCH AT THE BOTTOM OF THE NINTH WITH ONLY A ONE-RUN LEAD, NO OUTS, AND ALL THE BASES LOADED? I'D EASILY DIE!!
COME ON!

FIRST, GOTTA MANAGE TO TIE THE SCORE...
16
6

KILL

びくっっ
BIKU (JOLT)

ササーッ
SASAAA (SLIDE)

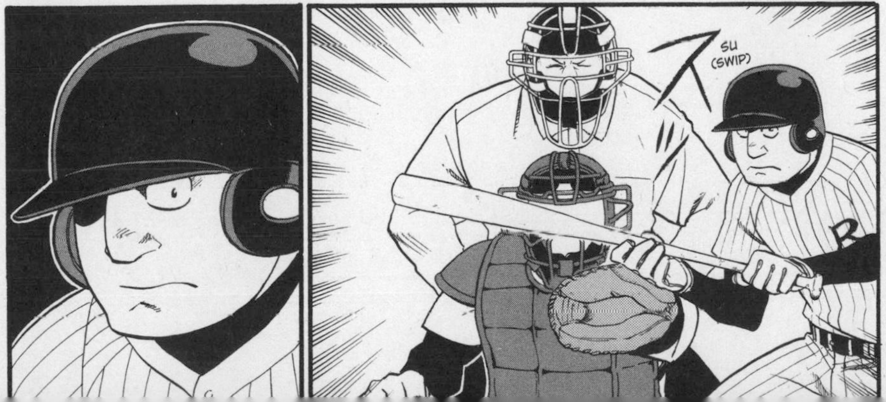

WHOA!!

DOPAN (WHAP)

STRRRIKE!

Silver Spoon

SHINICHIROU INADA
OBIHIRO KAWANISHI CENTRAL MIDDLE SCHOOL
FOOD SCIENCE PROGRAM, YEAR 3
TAMAKO INADA IN DAIRY SCIENCE YEAR 1 IS HIS LITTLE SISTER.

大蝦夷
WHUS WITH THAT FIRST-YEAR? HE SHORE THROWS A MIGHTY FINE PITCH!
KAAAA
THIS AIN'TCHER KANSAI. SPEAK STANDARD JAPANESE.
NO CHIT-CHAT.
Chapter 61:
Tale of Autumn
30

DON (BOOM)
KOMABA IS SOMETHING ELSE.
HE'S NOT SHAKEN BY THE BATTERS AT ALL.

GYAKII (KRAK)

GAH!!
BACHI (SMACK)
KAAAAAAAAAAAAAH!
TWO MORE !!
大蝦夷農
KIN (CLINK)
It's a popup fly ball to the catcher ...
He's out!! That's the second out!!

ONE MORE!

Number four, third baseman Iohara-kun.
RAAAAAAAAA

In the local prelims he had a batting average of .632 with four home runs...
...and just in this Hokkaido Tournament, he's had a batting average of .527 with three home runs!
WHO IS THIS MON-STER!?

RUN, KOMABA! RUN AWAY!!!
IF HE WALKS HIM WITH THE BASES LOADED, WE'LL END UP TIED.
GOT NO CHOICE BUT TO FIGHT.

MAYBE I HAVE NO RIGHT TO SAY THIS AS A SECOND-YEAR WHO'S LEAVING THIS TOUGH SPOT TO A FIRST-YEAR, BUT...

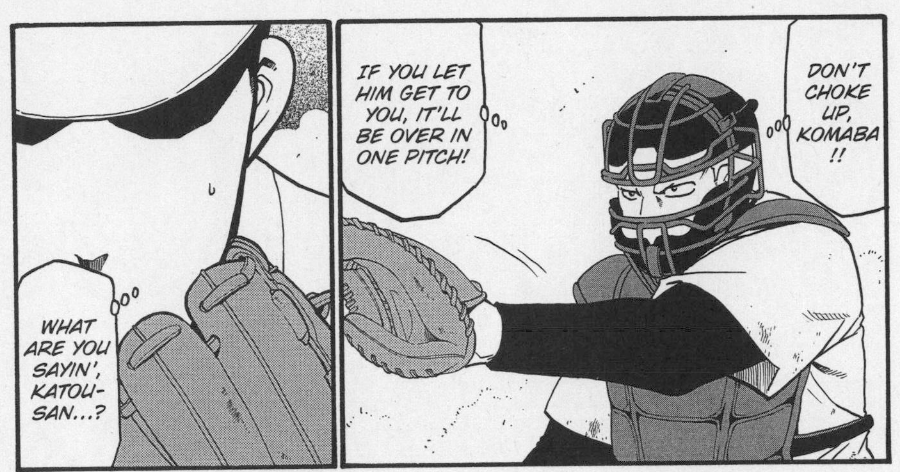

I AIN'T ABOUT TO LOSE!!

GO (WHOM)

GIN (CLANG)
It's a hit on the first pitch!!!
The runners all set off at once!!

ALL RIGHT!

It's a can of corn!

If right fielder Uryuu-kun catches this...

ビュ
BYU
(BWOOSH)
9 10 R H

Ahhhhh! What a shock!!!

TEAM 1 2 3 4 5 6 7 8 9 10 R H
EZO AG 0 0 0 2 2 0 0 1 0 5
RYUUHOKU 3 0 0 1 0 0 0 0 2 6
3 4 5 6 7 8 9
B
H

6

ざわ
ざわ
ZAWA
ZAWA
ZAWA
(CHATTER)

17

9

URYUU-SAN. I WAS ONLY ABLE TO GET THIS FAR PITCHING...
...BECAUSE YOU ALWAYS GOT HITS WHEN WE NEEDED THEM MOST.

THANK YOU VERY MUCH.

...I'M GOIN' TO THE CATTLE BARN.
AND I'M GONNA CHECK ON THE HORSES.

MORN-
ING.
HEY.

ZAWA (CHATTER) ざわ
DAIRY SCIENCE
1 – D
ざわ ZAWA
ざわ ZAWA

DID YOU WATCH THE SEMI-FINALS GAME?
YEAH, I WAS WATCHING IT LIVE!
ZAWA ざわ
ZAWA ざわ
WHEN THEY GOT THREE RUNS ON US IN THE FIRST INNING, I KNEW WE WERE GOING TO LOSE AND CHANGED THE CHANNEL.
ZAWA ざわ
ZAWA ざわ

WE WERE SO CLOSE!!
WE WERE TOTALLY GOING TO WIN!
WE MAY HAVE LOST, BUT OUR GUYS GAVE THEM A RUN FOR THEIR MONEY.

KOMA-BA WAS OUR STAR PLAY-ER!
YUP, WE LOST THE GAME, BUT HE WON HIS BATTLE!
HE PITCHED LIKE A GORILLA!

HERE WE WERE PLANNIN' ON HACHIKEN SHOWIN' US AROUND SAPPORO IF WE MADE IT ALL THE WAY TO THE FINAL GAME.
FORGET SAPPORO, FEELS LIKE WE COULD GO ALL THE WAY TO THE NATIONAL CHAMPION-SHIPS IN KOSHIEN NEXT YEAR.

ZAWA
ZAWA
HE'S RIGHT! WE'RE GOOD ENOUGH TO BE NECK-AND-NECK WITH A TEAM THAT GOES TO CHAMPIONSHIPS!
EXPECT GREAT THINGS FROM US NEXT YEAR!
WHY ARE YOU BRAGGING? YOU CAN'T EVEN MAKE IT ONTO THE BENCH.
WE'RE COUNTING ON KOMABA.

HUH? SPEAKING OF KOMABA, IS HE ABSENT?
NOW THAT YOU MENTION IT, I HAVEN'T SEEN HIM.

IS HE SICK?
ZAWA
ZAWA
MAYBE HE'S SPENT AFTER THE TOURNAMENT?

ZAWA
ZAWA
ZAWA

AND JUST LIKE THAT...

...KOMABA NEVER RETURNED TO OUR CLASSROOM.

Silver Spoon 7 • END

Silver
Spoon

His Best Feature

Don't Mess with the Straightedges

THEY WERE ON THEIR WAY TO LEAVE THEM WITH THE SHARPENER.

Cinderella Story

Cow Shed Diaries: Tale of the Irresistible Temptation

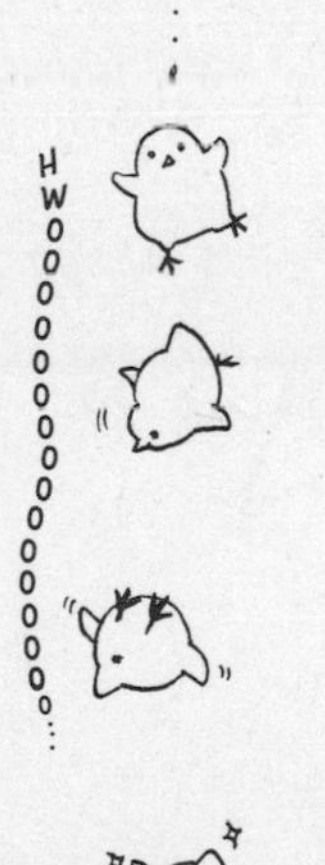

Silver Spoon 7!

Thanks so much for sticking with us through another volume! The Tale of Winter begins in the next book. Cold and harsh winter!

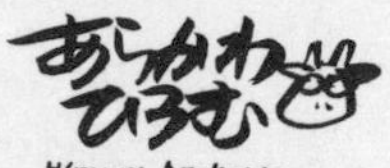

Hiromu Arakawa

~ Special Thanks ~

All of my assistants,
Everyone who helped with collecting material, interviews, and consulting,
My editor, Takashi Tsubouchi,

AND YOU!!

**A dream, shattered.
From his close proximity,
Hachiken can see it all.
His friend's frustration
and emptiness...
Hachiken is well aware that it
isn't his place to say anything.
Yet he can't back
down from this.**

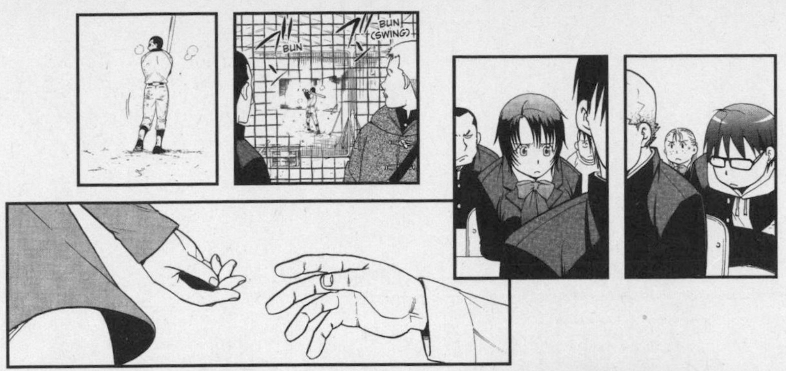

Determination dwells within the boy... And the seasons change again. Hokkaido winters are harsher than anywhere... Silver Spoon Volume 8 Coming April 2019!!

to be continued......

Silver Spoon

SECRET BASE

Translation Notes

Common Honorifics

no honorific: Indicates familiarity or closeness; if used without permission or reason, addressing someone in this manner would constitute an insult.
-san: The Japanese equivalent of Mr./Mrs./Miss. If a situation calls for politeness, this is the fail-safe honorific.
-sama: Conveys great respect; may also indicate the social status of the speaker is lower than that of the addressee.
-kun: Used most often when referring to boys, this honorific indicates affection or familiarity. Occasionally used by older men among their peers, but it may also be used by anyone referring to a person of lower standing.
-chan: An affectionate honorific indicating familiarity used mostly in reference to girls; also used in reference to cute persons or animals of either gender.
-sensei: A respectful term for teachers, artists, or high-level professionals.
-niisan, nii-san, aniki, etc.: A term of endearment meaning "big brother" that may be more widely used to address any young man who is like a brother, regardless of whether he is related or not.
-neesan, nee-san, aneki, etc.: The female counterpart of the above, *nee-san* means "big sister."

Currency Conversion

While conversion rates fluctuate, an easy estimate for Japanese Yen conversion is ¥100 to 1 USD.

Page 32
Takoyaki are grilled batter balls with octopus bits. Perhaps the ping-pong club chose them for their ball shape?

Page 36
Human sled teams ("*ningen banba*," literally "human draft horse") have their roots in Ban'ei races. It's not an original idea the Equestrian Club came up with, but rather another part of Hokkaido's local draft horse racing history.

Page 39
Oden is a common fast-food soup consisting of various ingredients, such as boiled eggs and fishcakes, stewed in a broth.

Page 47
The Battle of Sekigahara (1600) was a decisive battle fought by an Eastern army led by Hidetada Tokugawa's father, Ieyasu Tokugawa, and a Western army led by Ishida Mitsunari. Tokugawa's side was victorious, marking the beginning of the Tokugawa shogunate. Hidetada had been ordered to march his forces to Sekigahara to assist his father in the battle, but he arrived too late...

Page 56
"*Ichi*" means "one." Ayame is confusing the number that starts Hachiken's family name.

Page 83
Hachiken's classmates are listing off Sapporo tourist attractions. The Sapporo Clock Tower was built in 1878, is the oldest building standing in Sapporo, and has a museum. Hitsujigaoka (literally "hill of sheep") Observation Hill is known for its scenic view, the sheep that are allowed to graze there, and a statue of Dr. William S. Clark (1826–1886), an American professor who was invited to Japan to establish an agricultural college in Hokkaido. Finally, many events are held at Odori Park, and many other attractions such as the Sapporo TV tower are nearby.

Page 90
The Japanese name for the wish plaques is "*ema*," literally "picture horse," so this may be another reason for Ooezo Shrine to use a horse shape for theirs.

Page 114
Gundam is a mecha franchise featuring giant robots. The first TV series in the franchise, *Mobile Suit Gundam*, first aired in 1979.

Page 133
The people of the Kansai region (the southern-central region of Japan's main island, Honshu, where major cities Osaka and Kyoto are located) are very passionate about baseball, and the high school baseball championships are even held in this region. It stands to reason that the players from Kansai would be extra-good.

Page 147
The boy up at bat is speaking in Kansai dialect, thus the comment of the catcher—who responds with some Hokkaido dialect himself.

Page 168
The name on the business card is a play on the Japanese publisher of *Silver Spoon*, Shogakukan.

Page 169
Shabu-shabu is a savory hot pot dish made with thinly sliced meat and vegetables.

Translation: **Amanda Haley** Lettering: **Abigail Blackman**

GIN NO SAJI SILVER SPOON Vol. 7
by Hiromu ARAKAWA

Original Japanese edition published by SHOGAKUKAN.
English translation rights in the United States of America, Canada, the United Kingdom, Ireland, Australia and New Zealand arranged with SHOGAKUKAN through Tuttle-Mori Agency, Inc.

Yen Press
1290 Avenue of the Americas
New York, NY 10104

Visit us at yenpress.com
facebook.com/yenpress
twitter.com/yenpress
yenpress.tumblr.com
instagram.com/yenpress

First Yen Press Edition: February 2019

Yen Press is an imprint of Yen Press, LLC.
The Yen Press name and logo are trademarks of Yen Press, LLC.

Library of Congress Control Number: 2017959207

ISBN: 978-1-9753-2762-0

10 9 8 7 6 5 4 3 2 1

WOR

Printed in the United States of America